# contents

**Key**

Number and Place value

Addition and Subtraction

Multiplication and Division

Shape and Measure

Fractions and Decimals

Mixed Operations

# How to use this book

Read the instructions carefully before each set of questions.

Your teacher may tell you to GRAB something that might help you answer the questions.

Sometimes a character will give you a tip.

The first page of each section will have a title telling you what the next few pages are about.

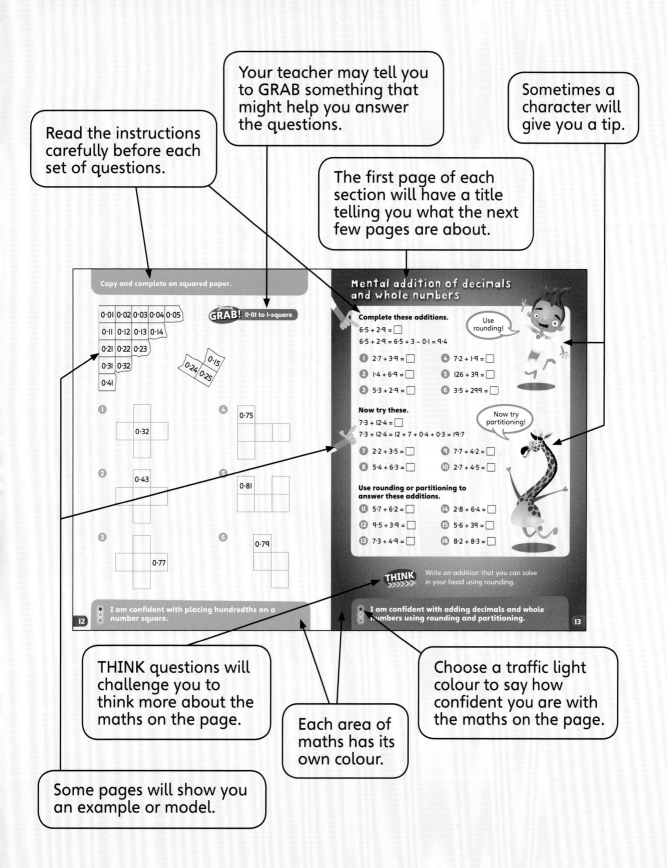

Copy and complete on squared paper.

| 0·01 | 0·02 | 0·03 | 0·04 | 0·05 |
| 0·11 | 0·12 | 0·13 | 0·14 |
| 0·21 | 0·22 | 0·23 |
| 0·31 | 0·32 |
| 0·41 |

GRAB! 0·01 to 1-square

0·15
0·24 0·25

① 0·32

④ 0·75

② 0·43

⑤ 0·81

③ 0·77

⑥ 0·79

I am confident with placing hundredths on a number square.

12

**Mental addition of decimals and whole numbers**

Complete these additions.
6·5 + 2·9 = ☐
6·5 + 2·9 = 6·5 + 3 − 0·1 = 9·4

Use rounding!

① 2·7 + 3·9 = ☐       ④ 7·2 + 1·9 = ☐
② 1·4 + 6·9 = ☐       ⑤ 126 + 39 = ☐
③ 5·3 + 2·9 = ☐       ⑥ 3·5 + 299 = ☐

Now try these.
7·3 + 12·4 = ☐
7·3 + 12·4 = 12 + 7 + 0·4 + 0·3 = 19·7

Now try partitioning!

⑦ 2·2 + 3·5 = ☐       ⑨ 7·7 + 4·2 = ☐
⑧ 5·4 + 6·3 = ☐       ⑩ 2·7 + 4·5 = ☐

Use rounding or partitioning to answer these additions.

⑪ 5·7 + 6·2 = ☐       ⑭ 2·8 + 6·4 = ☐
⑫ 9·5 + 3·9 = ☐       ⑮ 5·6 + 39 = ☐
⑬ 7·3 + 4·9 = ☐       ⑯ 8·2 + 8·3 = ☐

THINK  Write an addition that you can solve in your head using rounding.

I am confident with adding decimals and whole numbers using rounding and partitioning.

13

THINK questions will challenge you to think more about the maths on the page.

Each area of maths has its own colour.

Choose a traffic light colour to say how confident you are with the maths on the page.

Some pages will show you an example or model.

# 6-digit numbers

**Copy and complete these place-value additions.**

**1** ❪ 4306 ❫ – ❪ 200 ❫ = ❪ ❫

**2** 5735 + 60 = ☐

**9** 48 513 – 302 = ☐

**3** 3673 – 2000 = ☐

**10** 64 226 + 20 001 = ☐

**4** 9323 + 400 = ☐

**11** 88 976 – 740 = ☐

**5** 8562 – 6001 = ☐

**12** 96 818 + 2050 = ☐

**6** 2845 + 3030 = ☐

**13** 567 635 + 20 000 = ☐

**7** 77 635 – 5000 = ☐

**14** 875 969 – 60 000 = ☐

**8** 57 629 + 60 = ☐

**15** 344 873 + 5000 = ☐

 **THINK** Write a 5-digit number where all digits are the same. Now write a subtraction so that two of the digits become zero.

● ○ ○ ○ **I am confident with the place value of 4-, 5- and 6-digit numbers.**

## Write the numbers described in figures.

1. Five hundred thousands, three hundreds, eight tens, ninety-four thousands, six ones

2. Two hundreds, seventy-three thousands, seven ones, eight hundred thousands

3. Seven hundreds, twenty-four thousands, six ones, nine tens

4. Two hundred thousands, six tens, one thousand, nine ones, two hundreds

5. Eight hundreds, five hundred thousands, thirty-two thousands, six ones, four tens

## Copy and complete.

6. 743 913 – 900 = ☐

7. 502 889 + 4000 = ☐

8. 853 241 – 30 000 = ☐

9. 340 537 – 300 000 = ☐

10. 332 385 + 50 000 = ☐

11. 36 789 + 200 000 = ☐

## What number is:

12. 4 more than 49 997?

13. 100 more than 482 964?

14. 6 less than 200 000?

15. 1000 more than 469 305?

16. 1000 less than 400 478?

17. 7 less than 698 005?

18. 100 more than 89 995?

19. 8 less than 530 003?

 **THINK** If you are adding 100, think of three numbers where you will cross a thousand.

**I am confident with the place value of 6-digit numbers.**

## Write the numbers described in figures.

1. Six hundred thousands, seven hundreds, five tens, ninety thousands, three ones
2. Three hundreds, seventy-six thousands, four ones, nine hundred thousands
3. Seven hundred thousands, one ten, six thousands, five ones, two hundreds
4. Eight hundreds, two hundred thousands, thirty-six thousands, nine ones, three tens
5. Fifty-four thousands, three ones, one hundred thousand, five tens

## Copy and complete.

6. 674 907 − 500 = ☐
7. 145 786 + 4000 = ☐
8. 453 231 − 40 000 = ☐

9. 342 536 + 100 000 = ☐
10. 897 385 − 50 = ☐
11. 625 780 + 50 000 = ☐

12. ## Follow these instructions.

- Write a 6-digit number with no zeros.
- Write the complement to 999 999 by writing the matching digit to 9 in each column. For example,

$$574\,832$$
$$+\,425\,167$$
$$\overline{999\,999}$$

- Now find the digit sum of the first number by adding the digits until you reach a single digit number. For example,

$$5 + 7 + 4 + 8 + 3 + 2 = 29, 2 + 9 = 11, 1 + 1 = 2$$

- Find the digit sum of the second number. Record the two digit sums. Repeat this whole process five times starting with different 6-digit numbers. Write what you discover about the digit sums in each pair.

● I am confident with the place value of 6-digit numbers.

# Write the number of each tag.

**1**

342 000 — a   b   c   d — 343 000

**2**

164 000 — e   f   g   h — 165 000

**3**

500 000 — i (520 000)   j   k   l — 600 000

**4**

700 000 — m   n   o   p — 800 000

## Put these sets of three numbers in order, smallest first. Write a number that lies between the first two numbers and one that lies between the last two numbers.

**5**   357 886        836 412        771 352

**6**   563 585        523 994        565 003

**7**   283 111        278 584        219 268

**8**   828 921        827 663        828 699

● ○ ○ **I am confident with the place value and ordering of 6-digit numbers.**

9

# Decimal place Value

$3042 \div 10 = \boxed{\phantom{0}}$

| 100 000s | 10 000s | 1000s | 100s | 10s | 1s | • | 0·1s | 0·01s |
|---|---|---|---|---|---|---|---|---|
| | | 3 | 0 | 4 | 2 | | | |
| | | | 3 | 0 | 4 | • | 2 | |

## Work out the answers to these calculations.

1. $463\,500 \div 10 = \boxed{\phantom{0}}$

2. $472 \times 1000 = \boxed{\phantom{0}}$

3. $887\,530 \div 100 = \boxed{\phantom{0}}$

4. $5 \cdot 2 \times 1000 = \boxed{\phantom{0}}$

5. $905\,500 \div 1000 = \boxed{\phantom{0}}$

6. $3 \cdot 75 \times 1000 = \boxed{\phantom{0}}$

7. $943\,772 \div 100 = \boxed{\phantom{0}}$

8. $895 \cdot 34 \times 1000 = \boxed{\phantom{0}}$

9. $463\,532 \div 10 = \boxed{\phantom{0}}$

10. $27\,407 \cdot 5 \times 10 = \boxed{\phantom{0}}$

11. $130 \div 1000 = \boxed{\phantom{0}}$

12. $507 \cdot 02 \times 100 = \boxed{\phantom{0}}$

13. $3647 \div 100 = \boxed{\phantom{0}}$

14. $8785 \cdot 72 \times 100 = \boxed{\phantom{0}}$

## True or false?

15. If you multiply 34·6 by 100 you get 346.

16. If you divide by 10 the digits move one place to the left.

17. If you multiply by 100 the digits move two places to the left.

18. If you divide a 4-digit multiple of 100 by 100 you will get a whole number.

● I am confident with multiplying and dividing any
○ number from tenths to 6-digits by 10, 100 or 1000.
○

## Work out the answers to these calculations.

1. $664\,785 \div 10 = \square$

2. $97 \cdot 2 \times 1000 = \square$

3. $769\,531 \div 100 = \square$

4. $45 \cdot 64 \times 1000 = \square$

5. $95\,800 \div 1000 = \square$

6. $3 \cdot 09 \times 100 = \square$

7. $567\,256 \div 100 = \square$

8. $320 \cdot 75 \times 1000 = \square$

9. $83\,502 \div 100 = \square$

10. $895 \cdot 03 \times 1000 = \square$

11. $773\,593 \div 10 = \square$

12. $27\,407 \cdot 55 \times 10 = \square$

13. $4320 \div 1000 = \square$

14. $87 \cdot 01 \times 100 = \square$

15. $647 \div 100 = \square$

16. $5000 \cdot 72 \times 100 = \square$

17. $264 \cdot 7 \div 10 = \square$

18. $20 \cdot 09 \times 1000 = \square$

## True or false?

19. If you multiply 4·06 by 1000 you get 4600.

20. If you divide 308 by 100 you get 3·08.

21. If you multiply by 1000 the digits move two places to the left.

22. If you divide a 4-digit number by 100 you always end up with a 2-digit number.

 **THINK** Write a 3-digit number with two decimal places that when you multiply by 1000 has a tens digit of 7.

I am confident with multiplying and dividing any number from tenths to 6-digits by 10, 100 or 1000.

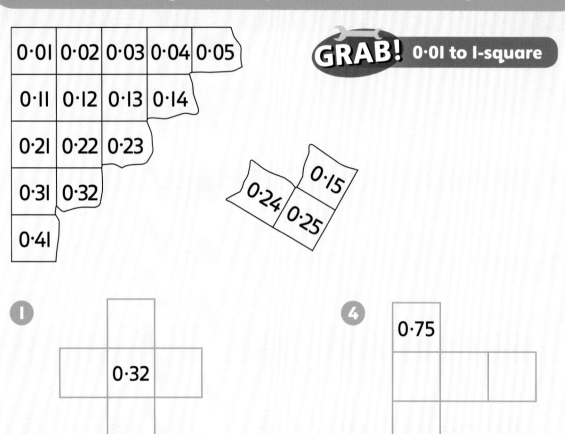

| 0·01 | 0·02 | 0·03 | 0·04 | 0·05 |
| 0·11 | 0·12 | 0·13 | 0·14 | |
| 0·21 | 0·22 | 0·23 | | |
| 0·31 | 0·32 | | | |
| 0·41 | | | | |

**GRAB!** 0·01 to 1-square

| | 0·15 |
| 0·24 | 0·25 |

**1**

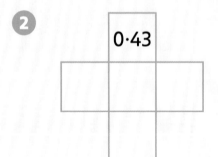

0·32

**4**

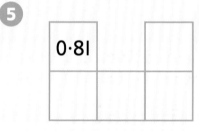

0·75

**2**

0·43

**5**

0·81

**3**

0·77

**6**

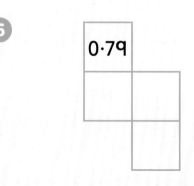

0·79

● I am confident with placing hundredths on a
○ number square.
○

# Mental addition of decimals and whole numbers

**Complete these additions.**

> Use rounding!

$6.5 + 2.9 = \boxed{\phantom{00}}$

$6.5 + 2.9 = 6.5 + 3 - 0.1 = 9.4$

**①** $2.7 + 3.9 = \boxed{\phantom{00}}$     **④** $7.2 + 1.9 = \boxed{\phantom{00}}$

**②** $1.4 + 6.9 = \boxed{\phantom{00}}$     **⑤** $126 + 39 = \boxed{\phantom{00}}$

**③** $5.3 + 2.9 = \boxed{\phantom{00}}$     **⑥** $3.5 + 299 = \boxed{\phantom{00}}$

**Now try these.**

> Now try partitioning!

$7.3 + 12.4 = \boxed{\phantom{00}}$

$7.3 + 12.4 = 12 + 7 + 0.4 + 0.3 = 19.7$

**⑦** $2.2 + 3.5 = \boxed{\phantom{00}}$     **⑨** $7.7 + 4.2 = \boxed{\phantom{00}}$

**⑧** $5.4 + 6.3 = \boxed{\phantom{00}}$     **⑩** $2.7 + 4.5 = \boxed{\phantom{00}}$

**Use rounding or partitioning to answer these additions.**

**⑪** $5.7 + 6.2 = \boxed{\phantom{00}}$     **⑭** $2.8 + 6.4 = \boxed{\phantom{00}}$

**⑫** $9.5 + 3.9 = \boxed{\phantom{00}}$     **⑮** $5.6 + 39 = \boxed{\phantom{00}}$

**⑬** $7.3 + 4.9 = \boxed{\phantom{00}}$     **⑯** $8.2 + 8.3 = \boxed{\phantom{00}}$

**THINK**    Write an addition that you can solve in your head using rounding.

○
○   **I am confident with adding decimals and whole**
○   **numbers using rounding and partitioning.**

**Complete these additions. Choose whether to use rounding or partitioning for each question.**

**1** 45·8 + 6·3 = ☐

**2** 29·9 + 8·2 = ☐

**3** 7·4 + 11·3 = ☐

**4** 163 + 29 = ☐

**5** 199 + 7·6 = ☐

**6** 7·5 + 5·2 = ☐

**7** 54 + 82 = ☐

**8** 39·9 + 5·6 = ☐

**9** 72 + 93 = ☐

**10** 4·4 + 12·5 = ☐

**11** 32·4 + 29·9 = ☐

**12** 217 + 198 = ☐

**13** 12·4 + 4·5 = ☐

**14** 16·4 + 24·2 = ☐

**15** 69·9 + 6·5 = ☐

**16** 25·4 + 7·4 = ☐

**Solve these problems.**

**17** In a rainforest two trees stand side by side. One is 34·3 m tall and the other is 7·6 m taller. How tall is the taller tree?

**18** A piece of string was cut into two pieces. One piece was 4·9 cm long and the other was 7·8 cm long. What was the length of the piece of string before it was cut?

 Two decimals have a total of 13·6. What could the numbers be?

I am confident with adding decimals and whole numbers using rounding and partitioning.

**1** At a weight-lifting competition, Jim lifts 34·3 kg. Dean lifts 4·9 kg more than Jim. How much does Dean lift?

**2** The winner of the competition lifted 18·3 kg more than Eva. If Eva lifted 32·6 kg, how much did the winner lift?

**3** Anderstall's football pitch is 67·7 m wide. Barnet United's pitch is 1·8 m wider than Anderstall's. How wide is it?

**4** Fortune Rover's football pitch is 70·4 m wide. Standarton's pitch is 0·9 m wider than Fortune Rover's. How wide is it?

**5** Bronsted's football pitch is 65·8 m wide. Chilten's pitch is 2·8 m wider than Bronsted's. How wide is it?

**This is a safe. Each number on it is a code.**

**6** Make an addition with two of these code numbers. Then write and complete all the possible additions of two codes. Can you prove you have them all?

**I am confident with adding decimals and whole numbers using rounding and partitioning.**

Answer these questions, using a similar strategy for the questions in each pair.

$36 + \boxed{\phantom{00}} = 100 \rightarrow 36 + 4 + 60 = 100 \rightarrow 36 + 64 = 100$

$2{\cdot}36 + \boxed{\phantom{00}} = 3 \rightarrow 2{\cdot}36 + 0{\cdot}04 + 0{\cdot}60 = 3 \rightarrow 2{\cdot}36 + 0{\cdot}64 = 3$

**1** $55 + \boxed{\phantom{00}} = 100$

$1{\cdot}55 + \boxed{\phantom{00}} = 2$

**5** $62 + \boxed{\phantom{00}} = 100$

$2{\cdot}62 + \boxed{\phantom{00}} = 3$

> Use your bonds to get to the next whole number or multiple of 10.

**2** $49 + \boxed{\phantom{00}} = 100$

$5{\cdot}49 + \boxed{\phantom{00}} = 6$

**6** $54 + \boxed{\phantom{00}} = 100$

$7{\cdot}54 + \boxed{\phantom{00}} = 8$

**3** $28 + \boxed{\phantom{00}} = 100$

$3{\cdot}28 + \boxed{\phantom{00}} = 4$

**7** $31 + \boxed{\phantom{00}} = 100$

$8{\cdot}31 + \boxed{\phantom{00}} = 9$

**4** $73 + \boxed{\phantom{00}} = 100$

$4{\cdot}73 + \boxed{\phantom{00}} = 5$

**8** $86 + \boxed{\phantom{00}} = 100$

$6{\cdot}86 + \boxed{\phantom{00}} = 7$

**THINK** If you know $0{\cdot}47 + 0{\cdot}53 = 1$ what other additions do you know? Can you write three more similar additions?

For example, $4700 + 5300 = 10\,000$

**What number must be added to each decimal to reach the next whole number?**

Use your bonds to get to the next whole number or multiple of 10.

**Copy and complete each statement.**

1. $5·71 + \square = 6$

2. $7·56 + \square = \square$

3. $3·47 + \square = \square$

4. $\square + 2·96 = \square$

5. $1·29 + \square = \square$

6. $\square + 5·82 = \square$

7. $\square + 8·74 = \square$

8. $6·19 + \square = \square$

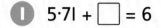

**Copy and complete each of these, counting up in steps to reach the answer.**

$4·35 + 0·65 + 4 = 9$

9. $16·27 + 0·73 + \square = 25$

10. $7·35 + \square + \square = 15$

11. $15·16 + \square + \square = 19$

12. $11·38 + \square + \square = 21$

13. $22·49 + \square + \square = 30$

14. $19·52 + \square + \square = 27$

15. $8·84 + \square + \square = 18$

16. $7·62 + \square + \square = 28$

**THINK**

$\square + 0·33 + \square = 19$

Give two different possible answers to this problem.

I am confident with adding decimals to find whole number answers.

**Solve these problems. Write each answer as a number sentence.**

Use RNCA to help you!

1. In a diving competition Clare scored 7·7 for her first dive and 5·9 for her second. What was her score altogether after the two dives?

2. Jamelia's score for her first dive was 2·5 greater than for her second dive. She scored 3·4 for her second dive. What was the score for her first dive?

3. Sara dived three times. She scored 5·7, 3·2 and 1·2. What was her total score?

4. In a javelin event Chloe threw a javelin 17·67 m. How much further did she need to throw it to get to 18 m?

5. In her next throw Chloe threw the javelin 18·34 m. How much further did she need to throw it to get to 19 m?

6. There were 8462 adults and 398 children in the crowd at the sports stadium. How many people were there in total?

7. At the stadium, John buys a packet of crisps costing 47p and a drink costing 85p. How much did he spend?

8. Kara ran 2 km in 236 seconds. Sam took 57 seconds more than Kara to run the same distance. How many seconds did it take Sam to run 2 km?

**I am confident with solving addition problems using mental methods.**

**Solve these problems. Write your answers as number sentences.**

Use RNCA to help you!

1. Fiona is doing a 2 km sponsored skip.
   After 5 minutes she has skipped 1·27 km.
   How much further has she to skip?

2. In a sponsored spell Class A raised £43. Class B raised £29 more than Class A. How much did both classes raise altogether?

3. In the sponsored spell, David correctly spells 38 more words than Jack and Jack correctly spells 17 more words than Simon. If Simon correctly spelt 32 words, how many did David spell correctly?

4. Lily raises £14·18. Her mum gives her some extra to make the amount up to the next whole pound. How much did Lily's mum give her?

5. Last year Bluebell School raised £4823 for a charity. By the end of January this year the school raised £759 more. How much has it raised in total now?

6. Bluebell School run a sponsored long-jump competition. John jumps 3·6 m and Lia jumps 1·7 m further than John. If Lia raises 10p for each 10 cm she jumps how much money does she raise?

7. The McNelly twins raised a total of £13·26. Each twin gives the same amount extra to make the total up to £14. How much extra did each twin give?

8. Two classes in the school collect old stamps. They are trying to collect 300 stamps. If one class collects 78 stamps and the other 165 stamps, how many more stamps do they need to collect?

○ **I am confident with solving problems using mental methods.**

**1**

Jumped from 2000 m

Opened parachute at 1750 m
How far did he freefall?

**2**

Jumped from 4000 m

Opened parachute at 2462 m
How far did she freefall?

**3** A rock climber climbs 22·7 m straight up a cliff face and stops to clip herself to a bolt. She then climbs up 5·4 m further. How high is the climber now?

**4** A bungee jumper jumps from a height of 7002 cm above the ground. The point at which he bounces back up is 6568 cm above the ground. How far did the jumper fall before the first bounce back?

**5** In a snowboarding slalom James travels at a speed of 32·4 miles per hour. His brother, Brad, travels 8·3 miles per hour faster than he does. At what speed does Brad go?

**6** A mountaineer climbs a mountain. He climbs a distance of 13·8 km before taking a break and then climbs a further 3·6 km. How far did he go in total?

**I am confident with solving addition and subtraction problems.**

**Solve these problems. Write each answer as a sentence.**

**1** A sky-diver jumps from a height of 5000 m above the ground. He free-falls down to a height of 4846 m above the ground and opens his parachute. How far did he free-fall?

**2** A mountain biker rides a 7000 m cross-country race. After 6274 m he gets a puncture. How far has he still to go to finish the race?

**3** In the same 7000 m race, Alan rides for 5734 m and collides with another bike. How far does Alan still have to go?

**4** Joe climbs a mountain with a summit that is 6003 m above sea-level. He stops at a point 5678 m above sea-level. How many metres above him is the summit?

**5** Keira is a kite surfer. In an attempt to break a record she kite surfed for 23 days. She hoped to reach 2000 km. Unfortunately she only managed to kite surf 1859 km. How much further did she need to kite surf to reach 2000 km?

**6** A snowboarder starts to go down a course that is 5010 m long. He falls at a point 3384 m down the course. How far has he still left to go?

**7** A scuba diver reaches a point 3008 cm below sea-level. He goes back up 2782 cm towards the surface when he sees a shark. How far does he have to go to reach the surface at sea-level?

**8** Felix jumped out of a plane wearing a wing suit. He soared for 7563 m and then opened his parachute. If the total distance of his journey was 9000 m, how far did he go with the parachute open?

○ **I am confident with solving subtraction problems**
○ **using the method of counting up.**

## Solve these problems. Write each answer as a sentence.

1. In a 7000 m cross-country mountain bike race, Jo rides for 4838 m before getting a puncture. How far does Jo still have to go?

2. Jo's mountain bike cost £1744. One of the most expensive mountain bikes in the world costs £3999. How much more expensive is it than Jo's?

3. A snowboarder starts to go down a course that is 5000 m long. He falls at a point 4384 m down the course. How far has he still left to go?

4. Six cavers go potholing and take a 5000 cm rope. They want to lower themselves into a 3754 cm deep cave. They fix one end of the rope at the top and drop it down. How much of the rope will fall on the floor of the cave?

5. Marik abseils down a 7000 cm rope and stops part way down, 5836 cm from the top of the rope. How much more rope has he left below him?

6. A different cave has a bottom 6007 cm below the surface. A potholer lowers himself to a point 4675 cm from the bottom of the cave and then goes back to the top. How far did he go, there and back?

7. A base jumper jumps from a height of 6008 m above the ground. He free-falls down to a height of 1656 m above the ground and opens his parachute. How far did he free-fall?

8. A triathlon consists of an 800 m swim, then a 20 000 m bike ride and finally a 5000 m run. After 1846 m Tanya had to stop with an injury. How far from the overall finish line was this?

**I am confident with solving subtraction problems using the method of counting up.**

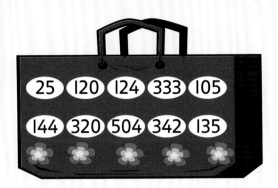

A number is divisible by 3 if its digital root is divisible by 3. A number is divisible by 4 if the 10s and 1s part of the number is a multiple of 4.

**Write the numbers in the bag that are divisible by:**

**1** 2

**2** 10

**3** 5

**4** 9

**5** 3

**6** 4

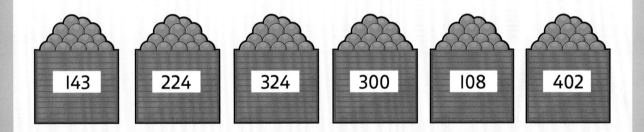

**Write which of these numbers of oranges can be put into:**

**7** packs of 3

**8** packs of 4

**9** packs of 3 and 4

 Think of a number which is a multiple of:

a) 2 and 9

b) 4 and 9

c) 3 and 5

d) 9 and 10.

● **I am confident with divisibility by 2, 3, 4, 5, 9 and 10.**

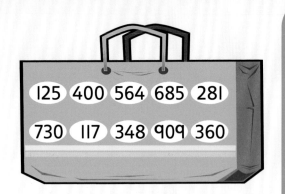

125 400 564 685 281
730 117 348 909 360

A number is divisible by 3 if its digital root is divisible by 3. A number is divisible by 4 if the 10s and 1s part of the number is a multiple of 4.

## Write the numbers in the bag that are divisible by:

**1** 2

**2** 10

**3** 5

**4** 9

**5** 3

**6** 4

## Write which of these numbers of doughnuts can be put into:

**7** packs of 3

**8** packs of 4

**9** packs of 3 and 4

224  213  711  612  708  897

## True or false?

**10** All multiples of 10 are multiples of 2 and 5.

**11** All multiples of 2 are multiples of 4.

**12** All multiples of 3 are multiples of 9.

**13** All multiples of 9 are multiples of 3.

**14** All multiples of 12 are multiples of 2, 3 and 4.

**I am confident with divisibility by 2, 3, 4, 5, 9 and 10.**

# Prime numbers and factors

| 1 | 2 | 3 | 4 | 5 | 6 | 7 | 8 | 9 | 10 |
|---|---|---|---|---|---|---|---|---|---|
| 11 | 12 | 13 | 14 | 15 | 16 | 17 | 18 | 19 | 20 |
| 21 | 22 | 23 | 24 | 25 | 26 | 27 | 28 | 29 | 30 |
| 31 | 32 | 33 | 34 | 35 | 36 | 37 | 38 | 39 | 40 |
| 41 | 42 | 43 | 44 | 45 | 46 | 47 | 48 | 49 | 50 |

1. On a 100-square, loop all of the prime numbers up to 50. Write how many there are.

2. Choose six numbers from the grid that are not prime and list all the pairs of factors for them. Try to find a number that has more than three pairs of factors.

 **THINK** Can a 2-digit prime number end in 2 or 4? Explain why. What digits can a 2-digit prime number end in?

- **I am confident with identifying prime numbers and factors.**

25

**Write all the prime numbers between:**

1  20 and 30

2  30 and 40

3  70 and 80

4  90 and 100

Are there the same number of prime numbers between each multiple of 10?

**Find all the pairs of factors for:**

5  27

6  36

7  45

8  64

9  72

10  51

**True or false?**

11  All prime numbers have exactly two factors.

12  All prime numbers are odd numbers.

13  1 is not a prime number.

14  Every 2-digit multiple of 6 is next to a prime number.

15  Every 2-digit prime number is next to a multiple of 6.

 THINK  13 and 31 are both prime numbers. How many other pairs of prime numbers with reversed digits can you find?

● I am confident with identifying prime numbers
○
○ and factors.

# Square numbers

**1** Draw the first square number, $1^2$.

**2** Draw the second square number, $2^2$.

**3** Write what was added to $1^2$ to make $2^2$. 3

**4** Draw the third square number, $3^2$.

**5** Write what was added to $2^2$ to make $3^2$.

**6** Draw the fourth square number, $4^2$.

**7** Write what was added to $3^2$ to make $4^2$.

**8** Draw the fifth square number, $5^2$.

**9** Write what was added to $4^2$ to make $5^2$.

**10** Keep going like this up to the 13th square number.

**11** Now write the 14th square number without drawing anything.

**12** Write $15^2$ and $16^2$.

**13** If $20^2$ is 400, work out what $21^2$ is.

**14** If $25^2$ is 625, work out what $26^2$ is.

You don't need to multiply!

 **THINK** Write a rule explaining how you find the next square number.

• **I am confident with square number patterns.**

# Dividing mentally

**Write each division.**
**Choose the correct answer from the list on the right.**

1  $450 \div 9 = \square$     90

2  $84 \div 3 = \square$     75

3  $360 \div 4 = \square$     32

4  $96 \div 6 = \square$     80

5  $128 \div 4 = \square$     50

6  $126 \div 6 = \square$     28

7  $114 \div 3 = \square$     16

8  $720 \div 9 = \square$     21

9  $145 \div 5 = \square$     29

10  $300 \div 4 = \square$     38

**Solve these problems.**

11  Chews costs 6p. How many chews can Max buy with 90p?

12  Li's dad takes 3 tablets each day. He has 111 tablets.
After how many days will he run out of tablets?

13  Four children are given £116 to share equally between them.
How much does each child get?

14  Eggs come in boxes of 6. How many boxes are needed for
420 eggs?

● I am confident with dividing by 1-digit numbers using
○ mental methods.

**Before answering these divisions, estimate the order of the answers from smallest to largest.**

**Now work out the answers to check.**

**1** 480 ÷ 8 = ☐

**2** 138 ÷ 6 = ☐

**3** 279 ÷ 9 = ☐

**4** 264 ÷ 4 = ☐

**5** 108 ÷ 3 = ☐

**6** 490 ÷ 7 = ☐

**Solve these problems.**

**7** Stickers come in sheets of 8. How many sheets of stickers does Ben have if he has 256 stickers altogether?

**8** An online photo album puts photos in rows of 4. How many rows of photos are there if there are 132 photos in an album?

**9** At Tonwell School there are 117 children. For sports day, the whole school is put into three equal teams. How many are in each team?

**10** A factory makes square picture frames from 4 equal lengths of wood. How many frames can be made from 476 lengths of wood?

Does 166 divide exactly by 8? If not, what would the remainder be?
Does 246 divide exactly by 8? If not, what would the remainder be?
Write other similar numbers that have a remainder of 6 when divided by 8.

● I am confident with dividing by 1-digit numbers using mental methods.

# Properties of triangles

**Write the name of each triangle. Choose from:**

isosceles                  scalene                  equilateral

right-angled scalene          right-angled isosceles

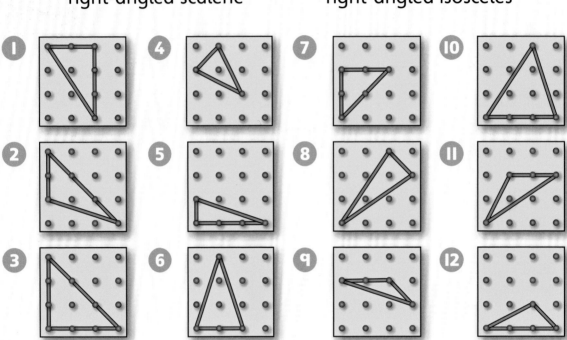

13  Which of the above triangles are symmetrical?

**Write true or false for each statement.**

14  A triangle cannot have more than one right angle.

15  Equilateral triangles have three angles.

16  A scalene triangle cannot be right-angled.

17  An isosceles triangle can be split into two equal
    right-angled triangles.

18  Isosceles triangles are always symmetrical.

19  Right-angled triangles are never symmetrical.

# Grams and kilograms

**Write the weight shown on each scale.**

**1**  —0 kg   1 kg—

**2**  —0 kg   2 kg—

**3**  —0 kg   5 kg—

**4**  60   kg   70

**Write each weight in grams.**

**5** 2 kg

**7** 11·3 kg

**9** 12·6 kg

**6** 3·5 kg

**8** 4·7 kg

**10** 30·4 kg

**Write each weight in kilograms.**

**11** 650 g

**13** 1010 g

**15** 1650 g

**12** 250 g

**14** 870 g

**16** 3040 g

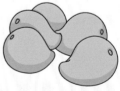

**THINK** Draw a scale that can weigh items that are all less than 250 g.

I am confident with reading scales and converting between grams and kilograms.

31

## Write the weight shown on each scale.

 1

2

3

4

## True or false?

5 3 × 350 g is more than 1 kilogram.

6 Each lump of butter is 2 g. There are five lots of 100 lumps in 1 kg.

7 5 kilograms is 50 thousand grams.

8 Half of 4·5 kg is 2250 g.

9 A horse weighs 1001 kg. This is more than one million grams.

10 1 kg of feathers is lighter than 1 kg of coal.

11 1·1 g × 10 multiplied by 100, is more than 1 kg.

**THINK** What is $\frac{1}{8}$ kg in grams? What other fractions of a kilogram can you find?

**I am confident with reading scales and converting between grams and kilograms.**

32

# Litres and millilitres

**Write each measurement in millilitres.**

① 4 l      ③ 0·2 l      ⑤ 0·25 l

② 0·5 l      ④ 1·4 l      ⑥ 1·75 l

**Write each measurement in litres.**

⑦ 3000 ml      ⑨ 1500 ml      ⑪ 2800 ml

⑧ 400 ml      ⑩ 750 ml      ⑫ 3250 ml

**Read each scale. How much is in each jug?**

⑬     ⑮     ⑰     ⑲

⑭     ⑯     ⑱     ⑳

**THINK** Write these measurements in order, from the least to the greatest:

500 ml   0·75 litres   0·2 litres   350 ml   1200 ml   1·4 litres

○ **I am confident with reading scales and converting**
○ **between litres and millilitres.**

33

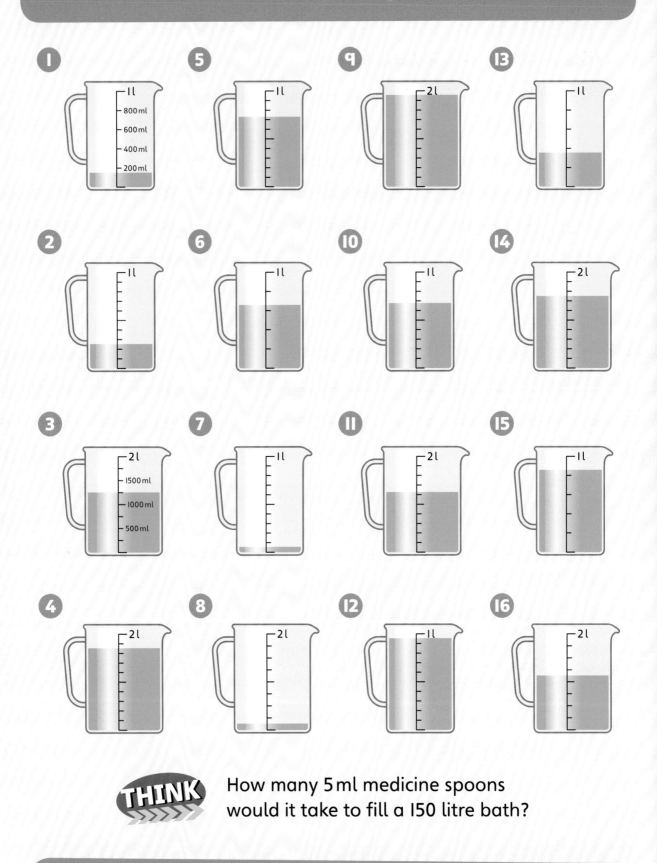

THINK How many 5 ml medicine spoons would it take to fill a 150 litre bath?

I am confident with reading scales and converting between litres and millilitres.

# Converting units of length

**Write each length in kilometres.**

1. 3000 m
2. 7500 m
3. 11 000 m
4. 250 m
5. 8700 m

6. 4200 m
7. 8760 m
8. 5010 m
9. 50 m
10. 101 m

**Write each distance in metres.**

11. 5 km
12. 13 km
13. 0·8 km
14. 4·3 km
15. 1·28 km

16. 0·08 km
17. 2·65 km
18. 5·735 km
19. 10·07 km
20. 0·004 km

**THINK** Use these cards in as many different ways as you can to make true statements. You can use more than one of each digit.

| 0 | 2 | 3 | · | m | km | = |

I am confident with converting between metres and kilometres.

## Sam has written a letter to her French penfriend.

Dear Claudette,
I have just returned from a brilliant school trip to an adventure camp. I am really tired though!
On Monday we walked 10 miles.
On Tuesday we cycled 15 miles.
On Wednesday we walked 12 miles.
On Thursday we paddled in canoes for 8 miles.
On Friday we cycled 28 miles.
Love Sam
xxx

**Use the graph below to help you convert each of the distances in the letter into kilometres, so that the penfriend will understand.**

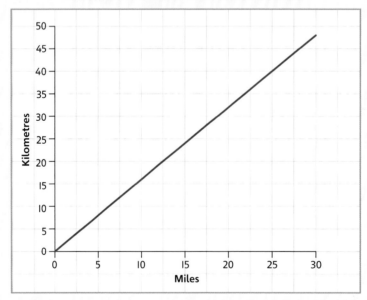

A graph to show the relationship between miles and kilometres

 Find the total miles for the week. Copy and continue the graph to work out how many kilometres this is.

○ **I am confident with converting between miles**
○ **and kilometres.**

# Adding 2-place decimals

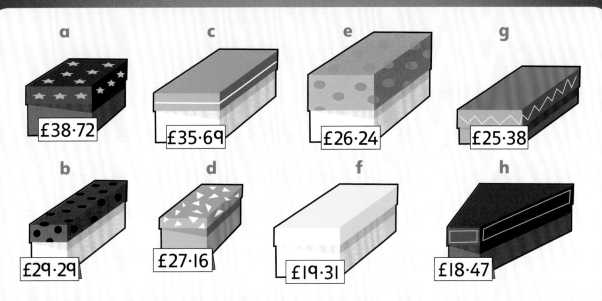

| | | | |
|---|---|---|---|
| a £38·72 | c £35·69 | e £26·24 | g £25·38 |
| b £29·29 | d £27·16 | f £19·31 | h £18·47 |

**What would the total cost be if you bought the shoes in boxes:**

1. e and f?

2. d and h?

3. b and d?

4. c and f?

5. d and g?

6. a and e?

7. g and h?

8. b and c?

**THINK** You have decided to buy this pair of shoes and the bag, and you want to buy the scarf. You have £30. Can you buy the scarf?

£12·83.

£10·69.

£6·39.

**I am confident with adding pounds and pence.**

£37·26
+ £45·63
_____

£37·26
+ £45·63
  |
_____
£82·89

## Perform these additions using the method shown.

**1**
£63·13
+ £33·78
_____

**4**
£33·28
+ £44·91
_____

**2**
£25·25
+ £56·72
_____

**5**
£47·06
+ £51·57
_____

**3**
£62·47
+ £25·43
_____

**6**
£26·59
+ £38·10
_____

## Perform these additions using the method shown.

**7**
23·14
+ 38·75
_____

**10**
38·52
+ 45·31
_____

**8**
67·24
+ 25·63
_____

**11**
23·59
+ 33·65
_____

**9**
13·29
+ 53·62
_____

**12**
47·06
+ 51·54
_____

**THINK** Choose a question from 1–6 and solve it as a decimal addition, without the £ sign. Will you get the same answer? Why?

**I am confident with adding two pounds and pence or decimal amounts.**

$$£81 \cdot 72$$
$$+ £12 \cdot 56$$
___

$$£81 \cdot 72$$
$$+ £12 \cdot 56$$
$$\underline{\quad 1 \quad}$$
$$£94 \cdot 28$$

## Perform these additions using the method shown.

**1**  £36·17
+ £54·31
___

**2**  £42·54
+ £53·62
___

**3**  £16·45
+ £27·42
___

**4**  £32·88
+ £54·31
___

**5**  £27·06
+ £44·53
___

**6**  £46·59
+ £82·13
___

## Perform these additions using the method shown.

**7**  28·13
+ 38·76
___

**8**  47·25
+ 25·61
___

**9**  13·29
+ 63·34
___

**10**  27·72
+ 51·31
___

**11**  27·53
+ 34·15
___

**12**  49·06
+ 51·53
___

**THINK** You have two prices to add together, and you know the total is £100. The total number of 10ps is greater than £1. What could the two prices be?

£ ☐☐·☐☐
£ ☐☐·☐☐

I am confident with adding pounds and pence or decimal amounts.

## Solve these word problems.

**1** A fork-lift truck is loading a lorry. It lifts a 46·75 kg crate onto the lorry and then lifts a 23·81 kg container on it. How heavy is the load on the lorry now?

**2** There are two crates to be loaded into a van. The smaller crate is 56·23 kg and the larger one is 18·42 kg heavier. How heavy is the larger crate?

## Answer these additions.

**3** £63·17 + £55·31 = ☐

**4** £82·79 + £43·40 = ☐

**5** £91·27 + £28·57 = ☐

**6** 76·78 + 78·51 = ☐

**7** 36·14 + 57·53 = ☐

**8** 66·62 + 52·42 = ☐

**9** 46·16 + 81·92 = ☐

**10** 86·77 + 52·51 = ☐

**11** 41·35 + 64·73 = ☐

**12** 83·37 + 84·59 = ☐

 The answer to this addition is more than 100 and it is a whole number. What could the missing numbers be?

£ ☐ ☐ · 3 7
£ 3 7 · ☐ ☐

I am confident with adding decimal amounts.

40

# Investigation

Two decimals are added together to give the answer 5·55.
We know two facts about the addition.

**Fact 1:** Only the digits in the hundredths column add to more than 10.

**Fact 2:** There is a '3' in the tenths column.

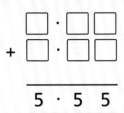

> The hundredths column will need to add to 15. It helps to write your bonds to 15 where both numbers are 1-digit numbers.

1  Find a way of making this addition work.

> Don't forget you can use '0' in the ones column.

2  Now find another way.

3  Find more ways and think about the answers to these questions:

---

4  How many different ways of doing this do you estimate there will be?

5  Can you work out how many ways of doing this there are in total?

6  Can you be sure that you have found ALL the ways?

7  Can you prove it to a friend or to the class?

---

⦿ **I am confident with adding decimal amounts.**

$6·7 − 4·76 = \square$　　　　　　　$1·7 + 0·24 = 1·94$

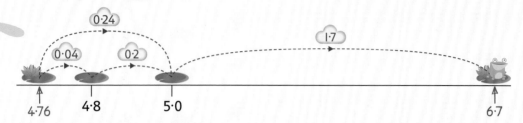

4·76　4·8　5·0　　　　　　　6·7

## Draw number lines to help you answer these subtractions.

**1** $13·2 − 10·54 = \square$

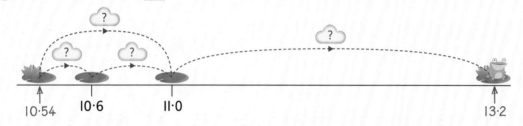

10·54　10·6　11·0　　　　　13·2

**2** $9·2 − 7·39 = \square$　　　　　**6** $10·21 − 8·63 = \square$

**3** $13·4 − 10·76 = \square$　　　　**7** $15·18 − 10·59 = \square$

**4** $6·1 − 4·18 = \square$　　　　　**8** $13·61 − 11·93 = \square$

**5** $11·5 − 9·66 = \square$　　　　**9** $18·72 − 12·85 = \square$

## Solve these problems.

**10** A length of wood is 3·63 m. Bob cuts 1·78 m off it.
How long is the length now?

**11** How much heavier is 14·2 kg than 11·87 kg?

**12** From Topton to Bury it is 13·32 km. Sanjar drives 7·64 km
from Topton towards Bury. How far has he still to go?

**13** Jo had £24·30. She spent £21·79. How much has she now?

**THINK** Write your own decimal subtraction
and draw a number line to answer it.

○ **I am confident with subtracting decimals by**
○ **counting up.**

## Answer these subtractions.

**1** $11 \cdot 42 - 7 \cdot 53 = \square$

**2** $13 \cdot 21 - 9 \cdot 74 = \square$

**3** $17 \cdot 23 - 13 \cdot 77 = \square$

**4** $24 \cdot 45 - 19 \cdot 28 = \square$

**5** $23 \cdot 34 - 17 \cdot 56 = \square$

**6** $22 \cdot 21 - 18 \cdot 88 = \square$

**7** $26 \cdot 34 - 22 \cdot 79 = \square$

**8** $46 \cdot 45 - 45 \cdot 56 = \square$

**9** $33 \cdot 23 - 29 \cdot 78 = \square$

**10** $21 \cdot 66 - 8 \cdot 32 = \square$

## Answer these word problems.

**11** The diameter of a football is 22·8 cm. The diameter of a tennis ball is 6·35 cm. How much larger is the diameter of the football?

**12** The area of a postage stamp from Ghana is 13·92 cm². It is 3·67 cm² larger than a stamp from New Guinea. What is the area of the stamp from New Guinea?

**13** Jack and his sister are raising money for charity. Jack raises £45·35, which was £13·21 more than his sister raised. How much did they both raise in total?

**14** Lia wants to buy a second-hand bike that costs £28·34. She has £18·56 in her purse and £8·21 in her money box. How much more does she need?

**THINK**

How many ways can you arrange the digits 1, 5 and 6 in the empty boxes to give positive answers? You may use each digit only once in a calculation.

$$5 \cdot 5 - \square \cdot \square\square$$

**I am confident with subtracting decimals using the method of counting up.**

43

Look at these questions. Estimate which will have the biggest answer and which will have the smallest answer.

Now work out the answers.

GRAB! Empty number lines

**1**   9·2 – 6·53 = ☐

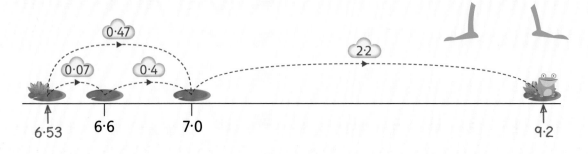

**2**   12·1 – 9·75 = ☐

**3**   16·4 – 14·87 = ☐

**4**   23·4 – 19·66 = ☐

**5**   9·11 – 5·84 = ☐

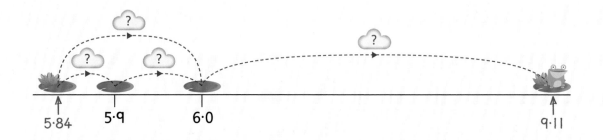

**6**   8·21 – 4·68 = ☐

**7**   15·11 – 9·77 = ☐

**8**   16·52 – 10·49 = ☐

**9**   29·13 – 25·81 = ☐

**10**   39·05 – 35·38 = ☐

○ I am confident with subtracting decimals
○ using the method of counting up.

## Answer these subtractions. Use jottings to help.

**1** 17·23 – 9·65 = ☐

**2** 22·16 – 10·48 = ☐

**3** 23·12 – 12·65 = ☐

> Remember, Frog jumps to the next whole number first!

**4** 32·07 – 29·38 = ☐

**5** 50·43 – 46·65 = ☐

**6** 35·64 – 22·77 = ☐

## Try these in the same way.

> Remember to add the smaller number to the bigger number!

**7** 8·15 – 4·72 = ☐

**8** 11·71 – 7·37 = ☐

**9** 16·64 – 9·59 = ☐   **11** 25·17 – 19·74 = ☐

**10** 18·36 – 14·74 = ☐   **12** 35·83 – 33·27 = ☐

 **THINK** Choose four subtractions on the page that you found hard. Check your answers to them using addition.

○ **I am confident with subtracting decimals using**
○ **the method of counting up.**
○

# Multiplying two 2-digit numbers

26 × 34 = ☐

| × | 30 | 4 | |
|---|---|---|---|
| 20 | 600 | 80 | = 680 |
| 6 | 180 | 24 | = 204 |
| | | Total | = 884 |

**Answer these multiplications using the method shown.**

1. 23 × 35 = ☐

2. 34 × 32 = ☐

3. 44 × 26 = ☐

4. 39 × 45 = ☐

5. 28 × 24 = ☐

6. 42 × 36 = ☐

**Now try these.**

7.  54
  × 34

8.  62
  × 25

9.  42
  × 19

10.  53
  × 74

11.  69
  × 17

12.  83
  × 45

 Is it true that if 24 × 35 = 840, then 35 × 24 = 840?
If 16 × 23 = 368, do you know what 23 × 16 is?

● I am confident with multiplying 2-digit numbers by
○ 2-digit numbers using the grid method.
○

## Write how much the coach company will receive on each trip.

**1** Mystery tour £32

27 people

**2** Sea and sand £42

18 people

**3** Lakes and mountains £56

33 people

**4** Famous gardens £33

32 people

**5** City of London £63

41 people

**6** Ancient castles £29

24 people

## Answer these multiplications using the grid method.

**7**   56
× 34

**8**   62
× 26

**9**   48
× 19

**10**   88
× 67

**11**   96
× 56

**12**   68
× 79

## True or false?

**13** 38 × 23 = 23 × 38

**14** 41 × 25 = (41 × 20) + (41 × 25)

**15** 26 × 30 < 36 × 20

**16** 36 × 27 > 37 × 26

**17** 18 × 24 = 14 × 28

**18** 19 × 72 < 70 × 21

**THINK** Does ab × cd give the same answer as ad × cb where a, b, c and d are all digits between 0 and 9? Try some examples to find out.

I am confident with multiplying 2-digit numbers by 2-digit numbers using the grid method.

# Dividing 3-digit numbers by 1-digit numbers

**Work out these divisions.**

**1** 3$\overline{)360}$

**4** 3$\overline{)306}$

**7** 4$\overline{)408}$

**2** 4$\overline{)440}$

**5** 6$\overline{)660}$

**8** 4$\overline{)480}$

**3** 3$\overline{)303}$

**6** 3$\overline{)330}$

**9** 4$\overline{)404}$

**Solve these word problems.**

**10** A factory has 630 eggs. They are packed in boxes of 6. How many egg boxes do they need?

**11** A field is full of sheep. If there are 804 legs in the field, how many sheep are there?

 **THINK** Cat has done three calculations and she has got all of them wrong!

$$\overset{21}{4\overline{)840}} \qquad \overset{11}{5\overline{)550}} \qquad \overset{22}{4\overline{)880}}$$

What has poor Cat done wrong?
Show her how to do these correctly.

○ **I am confident with dividing 3-digit numbers by**
○ **1-digit numbers.**

## Write out and answer these divisions.

**1**  4)448

**5**  3)639

**9**  4)884

**2**  4)484

**6**  3)963

**10**  4)848

**3**  3)369

**7**  5)555

**11**  3)693

**4**  3)633

**8**  3)999

**12**  7)777

 **THINK** Write a division with an answer of III.
Then write a division with an answer of 222.

## Look at the questions below.

 **THINK**  Write down which will have an answer between 100 and 200, and which will have an answer of more than 200.

## Now answer each division.

**1**  4⟌456          **5**  5⟌585          **9**  3⟌948

**2**  4⟌852          **6**  3⟌975          **10**  6⟌678

**3**  6⟌696          **7**  5⟌595          **11**  4⟌836

**4**  3⟌642          **8**  3⟌387          **12**  3⟌687

 **THINK**  Write some different division questions with the answer 114.

● I am confident with dividing 3-digit numbers by 1-digit
○
○ numbers.
○

## Look at the divisions below.

 **THINK** Some of these divisions are going to have remainders. Choose two that you think will have remainders.

## Now work out the answer to each division.

**1** 4)836

**5** 8)856

**9** 4)859

**2** 8)896

**6** 3)924

**10** 3)620

**3** 7)798

**7** 6)696

**11** 8)836

**4** 6)648

**8** 5)587

**12** 9)987

 **THINK** Write some different division questions with the answer 123 r 1.

● ○ ○ **I am confident with dividing 3-digit numbers by 1-digit numbers, with remainders.**

**Write your estimate for each of these divisions. Then answer them.**

**1**   4 ⟌ 568      **4**   4 ⟌ 684      **7**   3 ⟌ 848

**2**   3 ⟌ 516      **5**   3 ⟌ 754      **8**   4 ⟌ 576

**3**   5 ⟌ 805      **6**   6 ⟌ 849      **9**   5 ⟌ 767

**Solve these word problems.**

> Some answers may have remainders.

**10**   Fruit bars come in packets of 4. If the factory has made 856 fruit bars, how many full boxes do they have?

**11**   Each minibus takes 8 children. How many buses will be needed to transport 962 children?

● I am confident with dividing 3-digit numbers by 1-digit
● numbers, with remainders.
●

## Write the answers to these divisions. Some answers may have remainders.

1  3 ⟌ 147

2  4 ⟌ 236

3  6 ⟌ 258

4  7 ⟌ 637

5  3 ⟌ 288

6  4 ⟌ 307

7  8 ⟌ 634

8  5 ⟌ 259

9  7 ⟌ 275

10  9 ⟌ 743

If the divisor does not go into the first digit of the 3-digit number, see whether it will go into the first two digits.

 **THINK**  Can you write a rule to explain how you can tell whether a 3-digit ÷ 1-digit division will have a 2-digit or a 3-digit answer?

● **I am confident with dividing 3-digit numbers by**
○ **1-digit numbers, with remainders.**
○

## Solve these word problems.

1. Stickers come in sheets of 4. How many sheets of stickers does Matt have if he has 856 stickers altogether?

2. Ben's rabbit, Jess, is ill. He must put 5 ml of medicine into her water bottle each day. Ben is given 635 ml of medicine. After how many days will the medicine run out?

3. Hannah pays 4p per minute for phone calls. She pays 632p for calls. How many minutes is this?

4. A machine fits wheels onto new cars in a factory. How many cars can be fully-fitted with 4 wheels if there are 649 wheels in total?

5. Eggs come in boxes of 6. How many boxes are needed for 777 eggs?

6. Each minibus takes 8 children. How many buses will be needed to transport 956 children?

7. A carpenter makes square picture frames from 4 equal lengths of wood. How many frames can be made from 478 lengths of wood?

8. At a restaurant each pizza is cut into six slices. If 282 slices were served one evening, how many whole pizzas was this?

Make up your own word problem for the calculation 686 ÷ 8 and answer it.

● ○ ○ I am confident with dividing 3-digit numbers by 1-digit numbers, with remainders.

54

# Finding fractions of 3-digit numbers

**Find these fractions.**

① $\frac{1}{3}$ of 69

$\frac{2}{3}$ of 69

⑥ $\frac{1}{3}$ of 336

$\frac{2}{3}$ of 336

> Use your answer to the first in each pair to answer the second.

② $\frac{1}{5}$ of 95

$\frac{3}{5}$ of 95

⑦ $\frac{1}{4}$ of 484

$\frac{3}{4}$ of 484

③ $\frac{1}{4}$ of 96

$\frac{3}{4}$ of 96

⑧ $\frac{1}{3}$ of 993

$\frac{2}{3}$ of 993

④ $\frac{1}{3}$ of 84

$\frac{2}{3}$ of 84

⑨ $\frac{1}{5}$ of 655

$\frac{4}{5}$ of 655

⑤ $\frac{1}{6}$ of 84

$\frac{5}{6}$ of 84

⑩ $\frac{1}{6}$ of 696

$\frac{5}{6}$ of 696

 **THINK** $\frac{2}{3}$ of ☐ is 18. What is $\frac{1}{3}$ of the missing number? What is the missing number?

○●○○ I am confident with finding unit and non-unit fractions of 2-digit and 3-digit numbers.

## Find these fractions.

**1.** $\frac{1}{3}$ of 426

$\frac{2}{3}$ of 426

**6.** $\frac{1}{8}$ of 336

$\frac{3}{8}$ of 336

**2.** $\frac{1}{5}$ of 725

$\frac{3}{5}$ of 725

**7.** $\frac{1}{9}$ of 648

$\frac{2}{9}$ of 648

**3.** $\frac{1}{4}$ of 684

$\frac{3}{4}$ of 684

**8.** $\frac{1}{3}$ of 813

$\frac{2}{3}$ of 813

**4.** $\frac{1}{3}$ of 435

$\frac{2}{3}$ of 435

**9.** $\frac{1}{7}$ of 462

$\frac{2}{7}$ of 462

**5.** $\frac{1}{6}$ of 852

$\frac{5}{6}$ of 852

**10.** $\frac{1}{8}$ of 976

$\frac{5}{8}$ of 976

> Use the first answer to help with the second in each pair.

 How many different fractions of £48 can you find, where each answer is a whole pound? For example, $\frac{2}{3}$ of £48 = £32.

**I am confident with finding unit and non-unit fractions of 3-digit numbers.**

## Answer these multiplications.

1.    816
    ×   4
    ———

2.    928
    ×   3
    ———

3.    471
    ×   4
    ———

4.    356
    ×   4
    ———

5.    589
    ×   3
    ———

6.    276
    ×   5
    ———

## Write the total number of miles each aeroplane flies.

**7** London to Paris

213 miles
7 trips

**9** Paris to Madrid

652 miles
4 trips

**11** Vienna to Dublin

821 miles
8 trips

**8** Rome to Berlin

734 miles
3 trips

**10** Milan to Amsterdam

513 miles
6 trips

**12** Barcelona to Zurich

525 miles
9 trips

● I am confident with multiplying 3-digit numbers by
  1-digit numbers.

## Work out the answers to these multiplications.

1)
```
  324
×   3
_____
```

2)
```
  126
×   3
_____
```

3)
```
  321
×   5
_____
```

4)
```
 1253
×    3
_____
```

5)
```
 2125
×    4
_____
```

6)
```
 1214
×    4
_____
```

7)
```
 1114
×    5
_____
```

8)
```
 3214
×    3
_____
```

## Solve these word problems.

9) How many legs do 416 cows have?

10) A second-hand garage has three cars for sale.
Each car costs £1240. A car hire company buys all three cars.
How much did they spend?

 Write three multiplications with answers between 1000 and 1200.

• I am confident with multiplying 3-digit and 4-digit
numbers by 1-digit numbers.

## Work out the answers to these multiplications.

**1**   2318
    ×   4

**2**   3247
    ×   3

**3**   5161
    ×   5

**4**   3027
    ×   6

**5**   4156
    ×   3

**6**   5159
    ×   4

**7**   2116
    ×   8

**8**   5913
    ×   7

## Solve these word problems.

**9** A pilot flies 1251 miles each day. How far does he fly in 4 days?

**10** A person eats 1922 calories each day for 3 days. How many calories is this in total?

**11** A forestry company is planting trees in 5 rows across a large area. If they plant 1163 trees in each row, how many trees do they plant altogether?

**12** A footballer earns £4207 a week. How much does he earn in 8 weeks?

**13** A factory makes 4066 mugs each day, 7 days a week. How many does it make each week?

- **I am confident with multiplying 4-digit numbers by 1-digit numbers.**

**Work out these multiplications and divisions.
Estimate each answer before you work it out.**

**1**    819
       ×   4

**2**    928
       ×   3

**3**    4⟌856

**4**    9318
       ×   4

**5**    3⟌381

**6**    6⟌690

**7**    7724
       ×   3

**8**    4602
       ×   5

**9**    5⟌195

**10**   8⟌496

 **THINK**    Check two divisions using multiplication.

● ○ ○ ○   **I am confident with multiplying and dividing 3-digit numbers by I-digit numbers.**

## Solve these word problems.

1. How many horse-shoes are needed to shoe all the legs of 723 horses?

2. Four boys in the Smith family are given £636 to share equally between them. How much does each boy get?

3. How many tins of spaghetti are there in 516 packs of 4 tins?

4. For a pancake recipe Kasim uses 215 g of flour per person. How many grams of flour does he need to make pancakes for 8 people?

5. At a school sports day some oranges are cut into quarters for the pupils. If there are 324 oranges how many quarters are there?

6. Maisy and Wilf are saving up to go to America. Maisy puts £96 into savings each month and Wilf puts £243 into savings each month. How much money do they have after six months?

7. Lauren pays 6p per minute for phonecalls plus a monthly charge of £32. During January she makes 1216 minutes of calls. How much does she pay in total?

8. Farmer Jack plants 144 cabbages into six equal rows. A week later he notices that 8 of the cabbages in one row have died. How many cabbages are left in that row?

# Properties of polygons

**Draw the shapes.**

1 Draw a regular polygon where all the sides are the same.

2 Draw a polygon where two sides are 8 cm, two sides are 4 cm and all angles are right angles.

3 Draw a polygon with two opposite acute angles and two opposite obtuse angles.

4 Draw a polygon with three sides and one right angle.

**Match each shape to its correct description.**

5   6 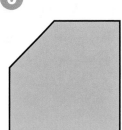  7 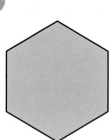  8

Description A  It is regular and has six lines of symmetry.

Description B  It has more than one pair of parallel sides.

Description C  It has exactly two acute angles.

Description D  It has no perpendicular sides and is irregular.

Description E  It is symmetrical and has two perpendicular sides.

 **THINK**  Draw a polygon. Describe the sides and angles it has.

○ **I am confident with drawing and describing**
○ **polygons.**

## Answer these questions on polygons.

**1** Define a polygon.

Remember to use the terms: acute, obtuse, parallel, perpendicular, regular and irregular.

## Name these polygons and describe them in terms of their angles and sides.

**2**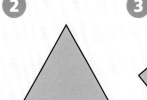

**3**

**4**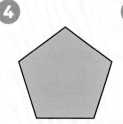

**5**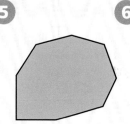

**6**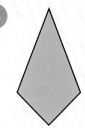

## Read the descriptions and draw the polygons.

**7** It is a triangle. None of its sides are equal but two of them are perpendicular.

**8** It is a regular shape that has only acute angles.

**9** It has three short sides and two long sides. It has three right angles and two obtuse angles.

**10** It has four sides. One pair of its sides is parallel. It has two right angles. None of the sides are the same length.

 Name some 2D shapes that are not polygons.

○ **I am confident with drawing and describing the**
○ **properties of polygons.**

**Write the name of each shape. Choose from the labels. For each shape, write the number of acute, obtuse and reflex angles.**

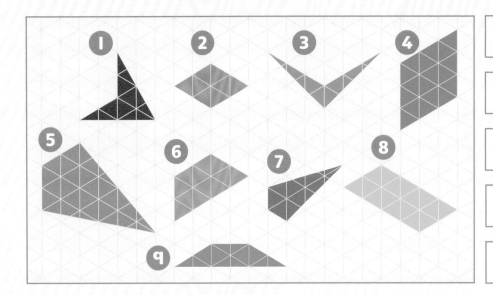

kite

rhombus

arrowhead

parallelogram

trapezium

**Write true or false for each of these statements.**

10   A kite has two pairs of equal sides.

11   An arrowhead can have a right angle.

12   An arrowhead has two pairs of equal sides.

13   An arrowhead has a reflex angle.

14   A kite need not be symmetrical.

15   A kite always has one pair of parallel sides.

16   A kite always has two pairs of equal angles.

17   If you draw a kite and make all sides equal, it is a rhombus.

18   An arrowhead has a line of symmetry.

 **THINK**   Draw a parallelogram and a rhombus. Describe the difference.

● I am confident with naming and describing
○ quadrilaterals.
○

66

**Copy and complete the table. For each statement and shape, colour the box the correct colour.**

|  | square | rectangle | parallelogram | rhombus | trapezium | kite | arrowhead |
|---|---|---|---|---|---|---|---|
| Has 4 sides |  |  |  |  |  |  |  |
| Has all sides the same length |  |  |  |  |  |  |  |
| Has only one pair of parallel sides |  |  |  |  |  |  |  |
| Has two pairs of parallel sides |  |  |  |  |  |  |  |
| Has opposite sides equal |  |  |  |  |  |  |  |
| Has adjacent sides equal |  |  |  |  |  |  |  |
| Has line symmetry |  |  |  |  |  |  |  |
| Has a right angle |  |  |  |  |  |  |  |
| Has an obtuse angle |  |  |  |  |  |  |  |
| Has a reflex angle |  |  |  |  |  |  |  |

☐ always true   ☐ sometimes true   ■ never true

 **THINK** For each of the quadrilaterals listed above visualise the diagonals – the straight lines going from corner to corner. Write whether the diagonals meet at right angles and/or whether they cross at their midpoints. Think about whether this will always be the same for each of the shapes.

● **I am confident with the properties of quadrilaterals.**

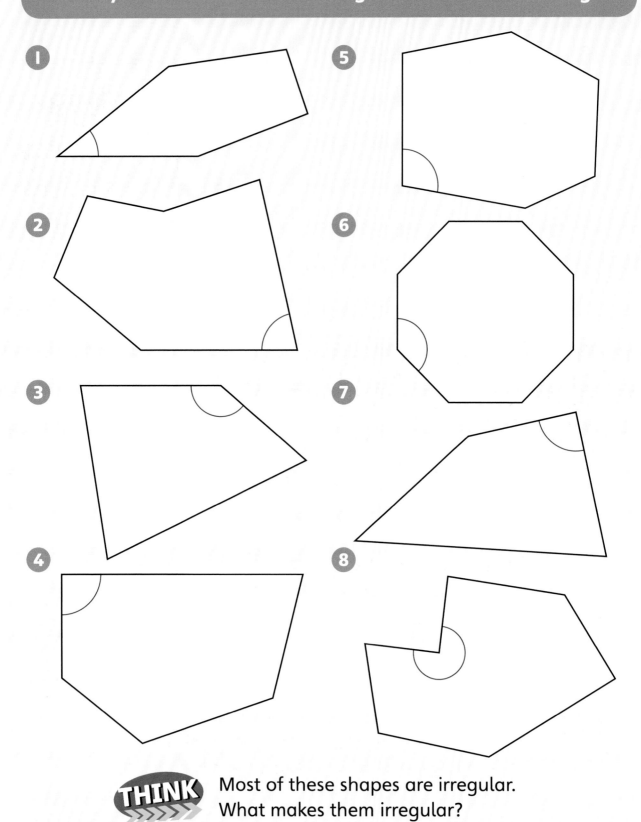

THINK
Most of these shapes are irregular.
What makes them irregular?

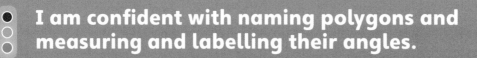

I am confident with naming polygons and measuring and labelling their angles.

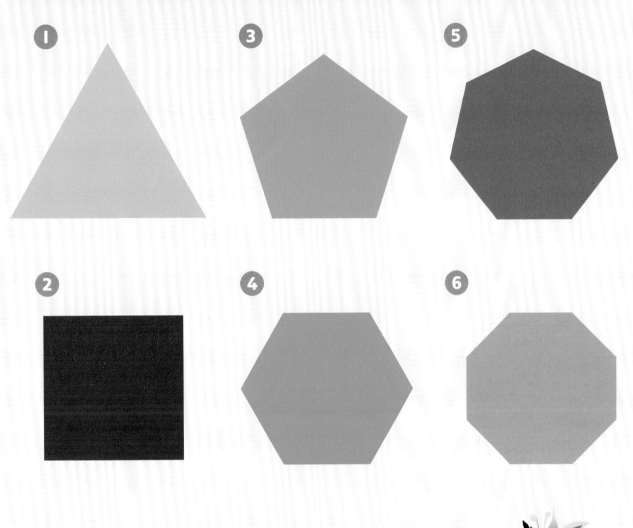

1

3

5

2

4

6

7 Look at your answers for the sum
of the angles in each shape. What
pattern do you notice in these totals?

 You have a 9-sided regular shape.
What is the sum of the interior angles?
What is the size of one of its angles?

**I am confident with measuring**
**angles of polygons.**

# Standard International and Imperial units

| Standard International units | Imperial units |
|---|---|
| metres / centimetres<br>kilograms / grams<br>litres / millilitres | feet / inches<br>pounds / ounces<br>pints / gallons |

**Match each Standard International measure to a picture. Write each equivalence.**

The baby is 3·5 kg, or 7 pounds and 8 ounces.

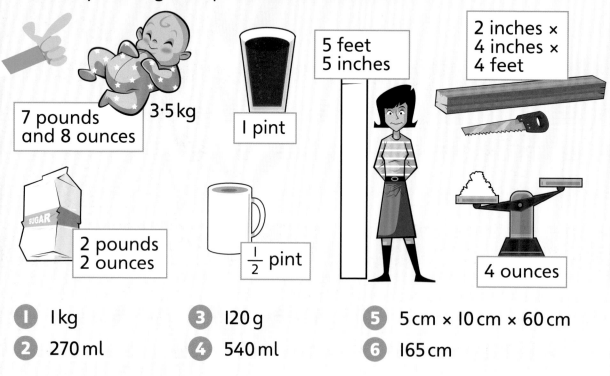

1  I kg

3  120 g

5  5 cm × 10 cm × 60 cm

2  270 ml

4  540 ml

6  165 cm

**Solve these word problems.**

7  Sam weighs 8 pounds when he is born. This is 3·6 kilograms. If he gains 400 grams in the first month, how much does he weigh then?

8  Lily is five feet and five inches tall. This is I metre and 65 centimetres. If her brother is 40 centimetres taller, how tall is he?

○ **I am confident with the relationship between Standard International and Imperial units of measure.**

| Standard International units | Imperial units |
| --- | --- |
| metres / centimetres<br>kilograms / grams<br>litres / millilitres | feet / inches<br>pounds / ounces<br>pints / gallons |

## Match each measurement to the pictures below.

**1** 7 pounds 6 ounces      **4** I pint      **7** 4 ounces

**2** 6 inches      **5** I pound

**3** 5 feet and 4 inches      **6** $\frac{1}{2}$ pint

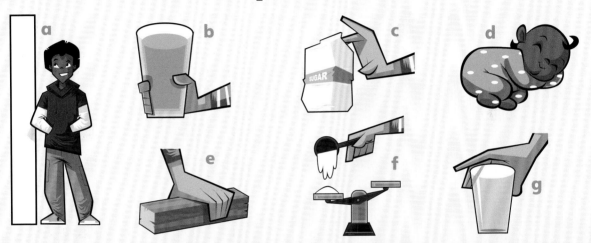

## Solve these problems.

**8** Deshi is born weighing 7 pounds and 8 ounces. There are 16 ounces in every pound and Deshi gains ten ounces in his first two weeks. How much does he weigh then?

**9** Emily is five feet and six inches tall. There are twelve inches in every foot and her brother is eight inches taller. How many feet and inches tall is he?

**10** Ian buys four pints of milk. If there are eight pints in a gallon, how many gallons is this?

 Do your parents or grandparents use Imperial units? Which ones? What do they measure with these units?

**I am confident with the relationship between Standard International and Imperial units of measure.**

# Mixed numbers and improper fractions

**Write the number of bars of chocolate as a mixed number.**

 ①

 ④

 ⑦

 ②

 ⑤

 ⑧

③

⑥

⑨

**Write the number of:**

thirds  $2\frac{1}{3} = \frac{7}{3}$ 　⑩ $3\frac{1}{3}$ 　⑪ $5\frac{2}{3}$

quarters 　⑫ $4\frac{1}{4}$ 　⑬ $1\frac{3}{4}$ 　⑭ $7\frac{2}{4}$

fifths 　⑮ $6\frac{4}{5}$ 　⑯ $4\frac{3}{5}$ 　⑰ $5\frac{2}{5}$

tenths 　⑱ $1\frac{3}{10}$ 　⑲ $3\frac{1}{10}$ 　⑳ $2\frac{7}{10}$

sixths 　㉑ $1\frac{1}{6}$ 　㉒ $1\frac{5}{6}$ 　㉓ $3\frac{5}{6}$

**THINK** How many whole pizzas could you have if you have between 20 and 30 thirds?

○ **I am confident with mixed numbers and improper**
○ **fractions.**

## Write each as an improper fraction.

1. $2\frac{1}{3}$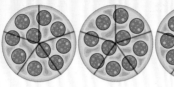

2. $3\frac{2}{5}$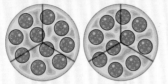

3. $1\frac{3}{4}$

4. $6\frac{4}{5}$

5. $2\frac{7}{8}$

6. $1\frac{7}{10}$

7. $3\frac{5}{7}$

8. $1\frac{5}{6}$

9. $4\frac{3}{8}$

10. $11\frac{2}{3}$

11. $8\frac{5}{9}$

12. $3\frac{8}{12}$

13. $7\frac{5}{11}$

14. $12\frac{5}{9}$

15. $6\frac{13}{15}$

## Write the missing numbers.

16. $1\frac{3}{5} = \frac{\square}{5}$

17. $2\frac{\square}{7} = \frac{18}{7}$

18. $3\frac{2}{3} = \frac{\square}{3}$

19. $5\frac{\square}{9} = \frac{49}{9}$

20. $\square\frac{3}{8} = \frac{51}{8}$

21. $\square\frac{3}{4} = \frac{19}{4}$

22. $8\frac{7}{10} = \frac{\square}{10}$

23. $2\frac{\square}{6} = \frac{17}{6}$

24. $\square\frac{1}{2} = \frac{9}{2}$

25. $7\frac{4}{5} = \frac{\square}{5}$

26. $5\frac{\square}{3} = \frac{17}{3}$

27. $\square\frac{2}{15} = \frac{47}{15}$

 Explore writing the number of weeks in 10, 20, 30 … and so on days as mixed fractions.

● **I am confident with mixed numbers and improper**
**fractions.**

73

# Investigation

**Work with a partner.**

> Always write a fraction in its simplest form. For example, $1\frac{2}{6}$ is $1\frac{1}{3}$.

**1** Write a mixed number of pizzas where the number of whole pizzas is 1. For example, $1\frac{3}{4}$.

**2** Write your mixed number as an improper fraction, a number of slices. For example, $\frac{7}{4}$.

**3** Look at the numerators (top numbers). Are both odd? Are both even? Is one odd and one even? For example, in $\frac{3}{4}$ and $\frac{7}{4}$, the numerators are both odd.

**4** Write a new mixed number, keeping the number of whole pizzas as 1. Write this as an improper fraction.

**5** Look at the numerators. Are both odd? Are both even? Is one odd and one even?

**6** Repeat this at least six times. Study the odd and even patterns in the numerators. Look at the odd and even patterns in the denominators. Write some rules to describe what you find out.

For example: If the denominator is odd and the numerator is odd, then the numerator of the mixed number is always …

○
○  **I am confident with mixed numbers and improper**
○  **fractions.**
○

74

## Copy and complete.

1. $3\frac{3}{4} = \frac{\square}{8}$

2. $4\frac{2}{3} = \frac{\square}{6}$

3. $5\frac{1}{2} = \frac{\square}{8}$

4. $3\frac{2}{5} = \frac{\square}{10}$

5. $4\frac{5}{6} = \frac{\square}{12}$

6. $3\frac{1}{3} = \frac{\square}{9}$

7. $2\frac{1}{4} = \frac{\square}{12}$

8. $3\frac{3}{8} = \frac{\square}{16}$

9. $1\frac{4}{5} = \frac{\square}{20}$

10. $4\frac{3}{4} = \frac{\square}{20}$

11. $2\frac{\square}{5} = \frac{24}{10}$

12. $3\frac{\square}{7} = \frac{50}{14}$

## Who am I? I can be more than one number!

13. I am a mixed number between 3 and 5. The numerator and denominator of my fraction part have a total of 6.

14. I am an improper fraction whose numerator and denominator are both odd and total 10.

15. I am a mixed number, in my simplest form. The total of the digits for my whole number part, my numerator and denominator is 9.

 **THINK** Use one set of 1–8 number cards. Use sets of three cards to make mixed numbers. Investigate how many different mixed numbers you can create between 5 and 7. Can you write them in order?

$$4 \frac{1}{5}$$

I am confident with mixed numbers and improper fractions.

# Multiplying proper fractions by whole numbers

Use number lines to help you work out the multiplications.

**Multiply these fractions. The first one has been started for you.**

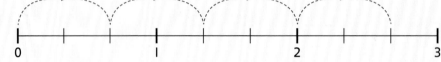

① $4 \times \frac{2}{3} = \square$

| | | | | |
|---|---|---|---|---|
| 0 | | 1 | 2 | 3 |

② $3 \times \frac{3}{4} = \square$

0     1     2     3

③ $\frac{4}{5} \times 3 = \square$

0     1     2     3

④ $4 \times \frac{3}{5} = \square$

0     1     2     3

⑤ $5 \times \frac{3}{8} = \square$

0     1     2     3

⑥ $\frac{7}{8} \times 3 = \square$

0     1     2     3

**Draw your own number lines to work out the answers to these questions.**

⑦ $\frac{3}{4} \times 5 = \square$          ⑧ $\frac{5}{6} \times 5 = \square$

**THINK**   $3 \times \frac{\square}{2} = 7\frac{1}{2}$. What number goes in the box?

○ **I am confident with multiplying proper fractions.**

**1** $6 \times \dfrac{4}{5} = \square$

0  1  2  3  4  5

**2** $\dfrac{5}{6} \times 7 = \square$

0  1  2  3  4  5

**Draw your own number lines to work out the answers to these questions. Write answers in their simplest form.**

Use number lines to help you work out the multiplications.

**3** $\dfrac{3}{4} \times 5 = \square$

**4** $6 \times \dfrac{2}{5} = \square$

**5** $\dfrac{5}{8} \times 4 = \square$

**6** $6 \times \dfrac{4}{9} = \square$

**7** $5 \times \dfrac{7}{10} = \square$

**8** $\dfrac{7}{8} \times 5 = \square$

**9** $6 \times \dfrac{5}{6} = \square$

**10** $\dfrac{7}{9} \times 3 = \square$

$3 \times \dfrac{\square}{5} = 1\dfrac{4}{5}$

What number goes in the box?

**I am confident with multiplying proper fractions.**

**Multiply these fractions.**
**Write the answer as a mixed number.**

$3 \times \dfrac{5}{7} = \square$

$3 \times \dfrac{5}{7} = \dfrac{15}{7} = 2\dfrac{1}{7}$

1. $3 \times \dfrac{4}{5} = \square$

5. $7 \times \dfrac{3}{4} = \square$

9. $9 \times \dfrac{3}{8} = \square$

2. $5 \times \dfrac{2}{7} = \square$

6. $7 \times \dfrac{5}{6} = \square$

10. $7 \times \dfrac{2}{9} = \square$

3. $2 \times \dfrac{5}{9} = \square$

7. $3 \times \dfrac{7}{10} = \square$

11. $9 \times \dfrac{3}{5} = \square$

4. $7 \times \dfrac{7}{8} = \square$

8. $8 \times \dfrac{4}{9} = \square$

12. $8 \times \dfrac{6}{7} = \square$

**THINK** Think of a multiplication of a fraction by a whole number where the answer is a whole number.

**I am confident with multiplying proper fractions and writing them as mixed numbers.**

**Multiply these fractions.**
**Write the answer as a mixed number.**
**Simplify your answers where you can.**

**1** $4 \times \dfrac{4}{5} = \square$

**2** $8 \times \dfrac{2}{7} = \square$

**3** $3 \times \dfrac{5}{9} = \square$

**4** $6 \times \dfrac{7}{8} = \square$

**5** $9 \times \dfrac{2}{3} = \square$

**6** $6 \times \dfrac{5}{8} = \square$

**7** $8 \times \dfrac{3}{4} = \square$

**8** $8 \times \dfrac{5}{6} = \square$

**9** $8 \times \dfrac{7}{10} = \square$

**10** $12 \times \dfrac{4}{9} = \square$

**11** $11 \times \dfrac{3}{10} = \square$

**12** $10 \times \dfrac{5}{6} = \square$

**13** $12 \times \dfrac{3}{8} = \square$

**14** $11 \times \dfrac{2}{9} = \square$

**15** $20 \times \dfrac{3}{5} = \square$

**16** $7 \times \dfrac{6}{7} = \square$

**17** $30 \times \dfrac{1}{8} = \square$

**18** $4 \times \dfrac{7}{12} = \square$

 Think of three multiplications of a fraction by a whole number where the answer is 4.

● I am confident with multiplying proper
○ fractions, writing them as mixed numbers
○ and simplifying them.

79

# Subtracting 4-digit numbers

**Write the answers to these subtractions.**

| | | | | | |
|---|---|---|---|---|---|
| **1** | 8527 <br> − 5363 | **6** | 4814 <br> − 2565 | **11** | 8276 <br> − 3854 |

**1**   8527      **6**   4814      **11**   8276
− 5363      − 2565      − 3854

**2**   9482      **7**   8218      **12**   6373
− 4645      − 6877      − 2384

**3**   8348      **8**   9380      **13**   8835
− 3662      − 4751      − 769

**4**   7275      **9**   6183      **14**   9123
− 359      − 2774      − 2487

**5**   5681      **10**   7264      **15**   8156
− 2394      − 2854      − 4467

**THINK**

What 4-digit number will make this subtraction work?

```
  3 1 0 5
− □ □ □ □
  1 2 8 9
```

○○○○ **I am confident with column subtraction of 3-digit and 4-digit numbers.**

## Perform these subtractions using this method.

| | | | **700** | **130** | | | | | | **7 13** |
|---|---|---|---|---|---|---|---|---|---|---|
| 8836 | | 8000 | ~~800~~ | ~~30~~ | 6 | | | | | 8 8 ~~3~~ 6 |
| − 1592 | − | 1000 | 500 | 90 | 2 | | | | − | 1 5 9 2 |
| | | 7000 | 200 | 40 | 4 | = 7244 | | | | 7 2 4 4 |

**1)** 8927 − 2565

**2)** 5562 − 2347

**3)** 9185 − 1663

**4)** 6944 − 5863

**5)** 8481 − 3934

**6)** 7785 − 1967

**7)** 8427 − 3663

**8)** 7114 − 2563

| | | | | **130** | | | | | | **13** |
|---|---|---|---|---|---|---|---|---|---|---|
| | | | **800** | ~~30~~ | **11** | | | | | 8 ~~3~~ 11 |
| 9941 | | 9000 | ~~900~~ | ~~40~~ | ~~1~~ | | | | | 9 ~~9~~ ~~4~~ ~~1~~ |
| − 2745 | − | 2000 | 700 | 40 | 5 | | | | − | 2 7 4 5 |
| | | 7000 | 100 | 40 | 6 | = 7196 | | | | 7 1 9 6 |

**9)** 8342 − 1685

**10)** 7352 − 5483

**11)** 6213 − 2565

**12)** 9646 − 7777

**THINK**

☐ 9 9 ☐ − 1889 = ☐

Write some possible digit numbers to go in the boxes and work out the answer.

**I am confident with column subtraction of 4-digit numbers.**

## Perform these subtractions using the column method.

(1)      8371
      −  5838

(2)      9411
      −  4275

(3)      8258
      −  3482

(4)      7273
      −  5957

(5)      5231
      −  2394

(6)      4314
      −  2565

(7)      8096
      −  6877

(8)      9324
      −  4759

(9)      6143
      −  2874

(10)     7264
      −  2877

(11)     8276
      −  3679

(12)     6373
      −  2984

(13)     8835
      −  3969

(14)     9365
      −  2487

(15)     8461
      −  4467

> Remember to write them out neatly, allowing space between the columns for moving digits!

## Solve these word problems.

(16) Joe bought a car for £3285. He sold it six months later for £1549. How much money has Joe lost?

(17) Nadine scores 8092 on a computer game. Her brother Talek only scores 7208. How many more points does he need to match her score?

 **THINK**  Choose one of the harder subtractions to do using Frog. Which method do you prefer and why?

○ **I am confident with column subtraction of 4-digit numbers.**

## Write the answers to these subtractions.

> Remember to write them out neatly, allowing space between the columns for moving digits!

| | | |
|---|---|---|
| **1**    7343<br>– 6868 | **6**    4274<br>– 2485 | **11**    8256<br>– 3857 |
| **2**    8576<br>– 3977 | **7**    8212<br>– 6877 | **12**    6311<br>– 2384 |
| **3**    9244<br>– 3687 | **8**    9340<br>– 4751 | **13**    8135<br>– 7769 |
| **4**    7114<br>– 5359 | **9**    6123<br>– 2774 | **14**    9223<br>– 2487 |
| **5**    6340<br>– 4872 | **10**    8336<br>– 4879 | **15**    6251<br>– 2554 |

## True or false?

**16** Subtracting a number ending in 9 always means you have to move a 10.

**17** Moving a 100 means the number of 10s in the smaller number is larger than the number of 10s in the larger number.

**18** Subtracting a 4-digit number from a multiple of 1000 always involves moving a 10, a 100 and a 1000.

**THINK** Write a good tip for a partner who is solving these subtractions to help them get all of the answers right.

○ **I am confident with column subtraction of 4-digit numbers.**

83

**Choose to use Frog or column subtraction to work out these subtractions.**

1)
```
   6724
 − 3561
```

2)
```
   4006
 − 2789
```

3)
```
   5228
 − 3416
```

4)
```
   9874
 − 2513
```

5)
```
   5023
 − 3684
```

6)
```
   8222
 − 4834
```

7)
```
   4562
 − 1238
```

8)
```
   9000
 − 6523
```

9)
```
   8724
 − 6813
```

10)
```
   7201
 − 4687
```

Remember, if you have to move lots of digits, it might be better to use Frog!

I always use Frog when there are zeros in the first number.

 Choose three of these subtractions which you found a bit tricky, and check your answer using addition.

Add your answer to the number at the bottom. If you get the number at the top, you are correct!

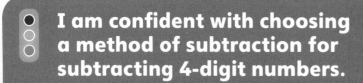

○ I am confident with choosing
○ a method of subtraction for
○ subtracting 4-digit numbers.

# Investigation

1. Write a 4-digit number made from a repeated 2-digit number, for example 9191.

2. Write it in reverse, for example 1919.

3. Subtract the smaller number from the larger.

4. Look at the answer, for example 7272.

5. Write it in reverse, for example 2727.

6. Subtract the smaller number from the larger.

7. Look at the answer, for example 4545.

8. Write it in reverse, for example 5454.

9. Subtract the smaller number from the larger.

10. Keep going like this, until you reach a 3-digit number and then stop! Make a note of the number you reach.

11. Try another starting number, for example 8282 − 2828 and keep going as before.

12. What patterns can you see?

13. Did you make the same number of subtractions to reach a 3-digit number?

14. Does the difference between the two digits in the number you start with make a difference?

I am confident with investigating the subtraction of 4-digit numbers.

**Estimate and then solve each subtraction using Frog or column subtraction. Check your answers using addition.**

Which method do you think was quicker for this subtraction?

4021 – 2678 = ☐     Estimate: 4000 – 2700 = 1300

$$
\begin{array}{r}
4021 \\
-\ 2678 \\
\hline
\end{array}
$$

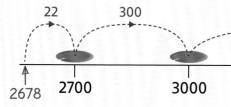

$$
\begin{array}{r}
9\ \ 11 \\
3\ \cancel{10}\ \cancel{10}\ 11 \\
\cancel{4}\ \cancel{0}\ \cancel{2}\ \cancel{1} \\
-\ 2\ \ 6\ \ 7\ \ 8 \\
\hline
1\ \ 3\ \ 4\ \ 3
\end{array}
$$

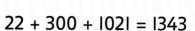

22     300     1021

2678  2700     3000     4021

22 + 300 + 1021 = 1343

Check by addition: 1343 + 2678 = 4021 ✔

1. 8342 – 5685 = ☐
2. 9042 – 5677 = ☐
3. 7124 – 3486 = ☐
4. 8274 – 2597 = ☐

5. 7002 – 5786 = ☐
6. 6302 – 5547 = ☐
7. 9452 – 5654 = ☐
8. 6010 – 3128 = ☐

 Which method did you use the most? Why?

I am confident with choosing a method of subtraction for subtracting 4-digit numbers and checking the answers with addition.

# Adding several numbers

**Copy and complete these tower additions.**

```
  3 4 2
  2 8 4
+ 3 9 8
  2 1
-------
1 0 2 4
```

**1**
```
   37
   45
+  63
----
```

**2**
```
   56
   39
+  48
----
```

**3**
```
   77
   81
+  94
----
```

**4**
```
   66
   25
+  19
----
```

**5**
```
   367
   345
+  263
-----
```

**6**
```
   156
   454
+  335
-----
```

**7**
```
   273
   835
+  197
-----
```

**8**
```
   329
   888
+  767
-----
```

**9**
```
   536
    45
+   63
-----
```

**10**
```
    62
    85
+  137
-----
```

**11**
```
   239
    83
+   77
-----
```

**12**
```
    68
   208
+   97
-----
```

**THINK** Draw a tower of three 3-digit numbers that adds to 999 in which there is one column where the digits add to more than 10.

○ **I am confident with adding several 2-digit and 3-digit numbers.**

## Copy and complete these tower additions.

**①**
```
    75
    88
    25
  + 63
  ____
```

**④**
```
    84
    57
    93
  + 88
  ____
```

**⑦**
```
   369
   548
   888
 + 261
  ____
```

**⑩**
```
   665
    45
   208
 +  63
  ____
```

**②**
```
    92
    65
    54
  + 48
  ____
```

**⑤**
```
   456
   854
   188
 + 337
  ____
```

**⑧**
```
   864
   353
   375
 + 976
  ____
```

**⑪**
```
  7668
   208
   208
 + 9887
  ____
```

**③**
```
    67
    25
    81
  + 94
  ____
```

**⑥**
```
   274
   228
   837
 + 196
  ____
```

**⑨**
```
   686
    78
   253
 +  97
  ____
```

**⑫**
```
  3576
   563
   278
 + 4789
  ____
```

## Solve this problem.

**⑬** Here are four of the tallest skyscrapers in the world.
What is the sum total of their heights?

828 m

601 m

509 m

492 m

**I am confident with adding several 2-digit, 3-digit and 4-digit numbers.**

**Look at the information about some of the world's tallest skyscrapers. Work out:**

1. the combined height of the top four skyscrapers.
2. the combined height of the top five skyscrapers.
3. the combined height of the bottom four skyscrapers.
4. the combined height of your three favourite skyscrapers.
5. how old each skyscraper is.
6. the difference in height between the tallest and the shortest in the table.
7. how many metres away each skyscraper is from one kilometre.

| Rank | Skyscraper | Location | Height | Date built |
|------|-----------|----------|--------|-----------|
| 1 | Burj Khalifa | Dubai | 828 m | 2010 |
| 2 | Makkah Royal Clock Tower Hotel | Saudi Arabia | 601 m | 2012 |
| 3 | One World Trade Center | New York City | 541 m | 2013 |
| 4 | Taipei 101 | Taiwan | 509 m | 2004 |
| 5 | Shanghai World Financial Center | China | 492 m | 2008 |
| 6 | International Commerce Centre | Hong Kong | 484 m | 2010 |
| 7 | Petronas Tower 1 | Malaysia | 452 m | 1998 |
| 8 | Petronas Tower 2 | Malaysia | 452 m | 1998 |
| 9 | Zifeng Tower | China | 450 m | 2010 |

828 m    601 m    541 m    509 m

492 m    484 m    452 m    450 m

**THINK** Draw a tower of five 5-digit numbers that adds to 99 999 in which there are two columns in where the digits add to more than 10.

**I am confident with adding and subtracting several 3-digit numbers.**

| Prices | Tablet | Smart phone | Hand-held console |
|---|---|---|---|
| | £539 | £510 | £307 |
| | £329 | £453 | £244 |
| | £186 | £175 | £185 |
| | £123 | £119 | £128 |

**You have won £1000 to spend in an electrical items shop. Solve the word problems.**

1. Choose one of each item which together you can buy for £1000.

2. Your friend has told you that the tablet costing £329 is the best. Which smart phone and hand-held console can you buy with that tablet for less than £1000? How much do you spend?

3. You get free minutes and texts with the smart phone that costs £510. Which tablet and hand-held console can you buy with that phone? How much do you spend?

4. The hand-held console that costs £307 comes with three free games, so you decide to buy it. Which tablet and smart phone can you also buy? How much do you spend?

5. You already own a hand-held console, so you decide to buy your mum a smart phone. Choose two phones and one tablet you can buy. How much do you spend?

6. The store manager says he can give you your change in cash. What is the largest amount of cash you can get, if you buy one of each item?

● I am confident with adding and subtracting several
○ numbers.
○

## Solve these word problems.

Remember to use RNCA to answer word problems!

1. 'Fun-tours' are running a three-day coach trip. Lots of people want to go so they use three coaches. 67 people go in one coach, 82 in another and 78 in the third coach. How many people go altogether?

2. The coach drivers fill up with fuel on the way. These receipts show how much they paid. What was the total fuel cost?

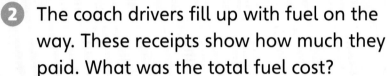

TOTAL : £61
TOTAL : £52
TOTAL : £87

3. 62 children, 96 women and 65 men pay to go on the trip. How many pay to go altogether?

4. Jo, Rob, Ben and Ella are running the trip. 'Fun-tours' give each of them some money for emergencies. Jo is given £75, Rob is given £42, Ben is given £53 and Ella is given £66. How much is this in total?

5. On Monday the coaches drive 78 km and stop for coffee at a stately home. Then they drive 86 km before stopping for lunch in a café. Finally they reach a hotel which is 84 km from the café. How far did they drive on Monday?

6. Chantel is on the trip. She spends £24 on Monday, £67 on Tuesday and £32 on Wednesday. How much does she spend in total?

7. On the return journey the coaches fill up with fuel again. They spend £77, £85 and £97. How much is this altogether?

I am confident with adding several numbers.

## Solve these word problems.

In a supermarket the self-service till weighs the items you buy. How heavy are these groups of items in total?

1. Jo buys 485 g of potatoes, 368 g of apples and 764 g of carrots.

2. Deepa buys 354 g of beans, 284 g of tomatoes and 695 g of carrots.

3. Eileen buys a box of washing powder weighing 2513 g, four tins of beans, each weighing 502 g, and 237 g of red peppers.

4. Jack buys two bottles of shampoo weighing 853 g each, three bars of soap, each weighing 87 g, and a jar of cream weighing 198 g.

   An electrician comes to check the three self-service tills.

5. There is £485 in till A, £378 in till B and £856 in till C. She removes £300 from each till to send to the office and closes them back up. How much is left in the three tills, in total?

6. Till A, containing £78, continues to be used for the rest of the day. Shoppers paying cash pay £37, £84, £66 and £114 into the till. How much does it contain now?

   > Remember to use RNCA to answer word problems!

7. A printed record shows that 5784 items were sold through till A, 7654 were sold through till B and 9564 were sold through till C. How many items is this altogether?

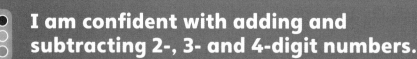

**I am confident with adding and subtracting 2-, 3- and 4-digit numbers.**

92

# Practising calculations

**1** 853241 − 30200 = ☐

**2** 887530 ÷ 100 = ☐

**3** 5·2 × 1000 = ☐

**4** 199 + 7·6 = ☐

**5** 16·27 + 0·73 + ☐ = 25

**6** 905500 ÷ 1000 = ☐

**7** 7·5 + 5·2 = ☐

**8**  £47 · 25
    +  £25 · 61
    ‾‾‾‾‾‾‾‾

**9** 13·4 − 10·76 = ☐

**10** $\frac{5}{8}$ × 4 = ☐

**11** 6·1 − 4·18 = ☐

**12**   7273
     − 5957
     ‾‾‾‾‾

**13**   67
      25
      81
    + 94
    ‾‾‾‾

**14** 16·4 + 24·2 = ☐

**15** 32 × 24 = ☐

**16** 130 ÷ 1000 = ☐

**17** 36789 + 202000 = ☐

**18** 22·49 + ☐ + ☐ = 30

**19** 507·02 × 100 = ☐

**20** 128 ÷ 4 = ☐

**21**   27 · 53
     + 34 · 15
     ‾‾‾‾‾‾

**22** 15·18 − 10·59 = ☐

**23** 6 × $\frac{5}{6}$ = ☐

**24** 13·61 − 11·93 = ☐

**25** 3 )‾638‾

**26**   3576
      563
      278
    + 4789
    ‾‾‾‾‾

**27** In a 7000 m bike race, Alan rides for 5734 m and collides with another bike. How far does Alan still have to go?

# Code puzzles

**This sentence is made with 2-letter words:**

"If my Ma is up on an ox so is Pa, or he is by it."

**1** Write this sentence in code.
Find the letters in the key below and add the two
numbers to give a total for each word.

| a | b | c | d | e | f | g | h | i | j | k | l | m |
|---|---|---|---|---|---|---|---|---|---|---|---|---|
| 381 | 204 | 296 | 191 | 327 | 562 | 333 | 477 | 229 | 144 | 243 | 181 | 435 |

| n | o | p | q | r | s | t | u | v | w | x | y | z |
|---|---|---|---|---|---|---|---|---|---|---|---|---|
| 566 | 244 | 391 | 556 | 248 | 317 | 239 | 346 | 691 | 582 | 564 | 475 | 497 |

| If | my | Ma... |
|----|----|-------|
| 229 + 562 = 791 | 435 + 475 = ... | |

**2** Write your own sentence using 2- or 3-letter words and
write them in code.

**3** Find the totals for these animals. Which of them have
the same total?

| cat | dog | hen | pig | fox | owl |
|-----|-----|-----|-----|-----|-----|

**4** Can you find a 3-letter bird name that has the total 1000?

**Use addition and subtraction to find the difference in the totals for these pairs of animal's names:**

5 a bat and an ape.

6 a rat and a cow.

7 a yak and a bee.

8 a gnu and an emu.

9 Write the numbers for each of the letters of your name in a tower and find the total.

10 Do the same for a friend or family member's name.

11 What is the difference between the two totals you have found?

12 Now find Alfred's total.

13 What is the difference between Alfred's total and your own?

| A | 3 | 8 | 1 |
| L | 1 | 8 | 1 |
| F | 5 | 6 | 2 |
| R | 2 | 4 | 8 |
| E | 3 | 2 | 7 |
| D | 1 | 9 | 1 |

Series Editor
Ruth Merttens

Author Team
Jennie Kerwin and Hilda Merttens

Published by Pearson Education Limited, Edinburgh Gate, Harlow, Essex, CM20 2JE.

www.pearsonschools.co.uk

Text © Pearson Education Limited 2013
Typeset by Debbie Oatley @ room9design
Original illustrations © Pearson Education Limited 2013
Illustrated by Andrew Painter, Matthew Buckley, Marek Jagucki, Anthony Rule, Debbie Oatley
Cover design by Pearson Education Limited
Cover illustration and Abacus character artwork by Volker Beisler © Pearson Education Limited
Additional contributions by Hilary Koll and Steve Mills, CME Projects Ltd.

First published 2013

16
10 9 8 7

**British Library Cataloguing in Publication Data**
A catalogue record for this book is available from the British Library

ISBN 978 1 408 27854 3

Printed in Slovakia by Neografia

**Acknowledgements**
We would like to thank the staff and pupils at North Kidlington Primary School, Haydon Wick Primary School, Swindon, St Mary's Catholic Primary School, Bodmin, St Andrew's C of E Primary & Nursery School, Sutton-in-Ashfield, Saint James' C of E Primary School, Southampton and Harborne Primary School, Birmingham, for their invaluable help in the development and trialling of this book.

Every effort has been made to contact copyright holders of material reproduced in this book. Any omissions will be rectified in subsequent printings if notice is given to the publishers.